M

D0835617

95 0296435 8

SS/ST

GO FACTS OCEANS

Coral Reefs

A & C BLACK • LONDON

Coral Reefs

contents

© Blake Publishing Pty Ltd 2002
Additional Material © A & C Black Publishers Ltd 2003

First published 2002 in Australia by Blake Education Pty Ltd

This edition published 2003 in the United Kingdom by
A&C Black Publishers Ltd, 37 Soho Square, London W1D 3QZ
www.acblack.com

ISBN 0-7136-6600-5

A CIP record for this book is available from the British Library.

Written by Katy Pike and Garda Turner
Science Consultant: Dr Will Edwards, James Cook University
Design and layout by The Modern Art Production Group
Photos by Photodisc, Stockbyte, John Foxx, Corbis, Imagin, Artville Digital
Vision and Corel

UK Series Consultant: Julie Garnett

Printed in Hong Kong by Wing King Tong Co Ltd

A & C Black uses paper produced with elemental chlorine-free pulp,
harvested from managed sustainable forests.

Coral Reefs

Coral reefs are found in tropical oceans around the world. Reefs are built up by small animals called coral polyps. The stony walls and platforms that polyps build, attract large communities of plants and animals.

Coral usually grows in warm, crystal-clear water. These conditions can be found in some shallow, **tropical** waters. In these waters large communities of coral grow in different shapes and brilliant colours.

Reefs provide food and protection for fish, **crustaceans**, starfish and **molluscs**. Reefs are also home to many different plant-like **species**, such as green, brown and red **algae**.

blood star and purple coral

There are three types of reef—fringing, barrier and **atolls**. **Fringing reefs** form close to shore, running along the edge of the land. **Barrier reefs** run parallel to the land but are much further from shore. They create a barrier between the deep ocean and the land. Coral atolls are rings of coral. Atolls form around the **lagoons** left by volcanic islands that have sunk back into the sea.

DID YOU KNOW?

Australia's Great Barrier Reef is the largest structure made by nature. It is so big it can be seen from outer space.

Marine life is plentiful on coral reefs.

Most coral reefs grow in sunlit zones.

Large barrier reefs are made up of thousands of smaller individual reefs.

What is Coral?

Coral polyps are tiny animals that live together in large, colourful colonies. They are soft-bodied animals with stinging tentacles.

Coral **polyps** are shaped like tubes. One end of a coral polyp anchors itself to the reef and the other end has a mouth. The mouth is surrounded by a ring of stinging tentacles that can catch food, such as tiny fish and floating **plankton**.

Coral reefs are built up from the stony skeletons of dead polyps. Each polyp lives inside a cup-shaped hole. Reef-building polyps make a stony outer skeleton to protect their soft bodies. As one polyp dies, another one grows on top. Only the outer layer of a reef is alive.

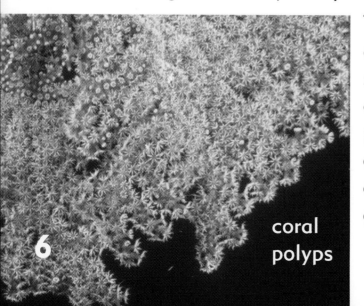

coral polyps

Tiny algae live inside each coral polyp. These plants supply the animal polyp with oxygen and food. Like all plants, the algae inside the coral need sunlight to live and grow. Reef-building coral grows in shallow, clear waters.

Coral polyps can pull
in their tentacles.

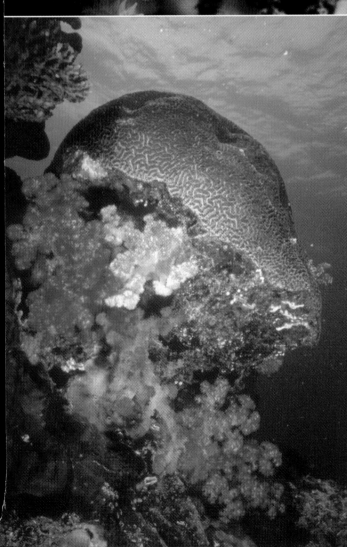

Reef-building corals have a
stony outer skeleton.

Left: Brain coral is a hard,
reef-building coral.

7

How Does Coral Grow?

Tropical coral grows in warm, clear, shallow sea water. A coral polyp grows from a small egg.

Life Cycle of a Coral Polyp

1. Adult coral polyps produce thousands of tiny eggs. This often happens at the end of spring or in early summer.

2. A **larva** hatches out of the tiny egg and floats in the water.

3. The larva attaches to the reef.

4. The larva changes into an adult polyp with a mouth, stomach and tentacles. A coral-forming polyp then makes a hard, outer skeleton to protect itself.

Types of Coral

Coral comes in all kinds of shapes and colours. It can grow into large, solid masses, tall fingers, or it can be soft and feathery.

elkhorn coral

fire coral

Soft fan coral sways with the movement of the water.

Plate coral looks like underwater trees.

Pillar coral grows like tall fingers.

The golden polyps of tube coral come out at night.

You can clearly see each polyp on this Gorgonian coral.

Sea sponges and coral often grow together.

Soft coral can be brilliantly coloured.

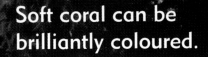
GO FACTS

DID YOU KNOW?

Coral reefs have been present on Earth for over 240 million years.

11

Life on a Reef

Teeming with life, reefs are home to nearly a million species of marine plants and animals. The widest diversity of sea life is found on coral reefs.

Food Chains on a Coral Reef

Marine plants are important on a coral reef. Many small fish eat algae or plankton. Coral polyps also eat plankton.

flame scallop

Crustaceans, such as shrimps, lobsters and crabs, eat dead animals and other things on the sea floor.

Larger fish, such as goatfish and butterflyfish, eat the smaller fish and crustaceans. Octopuses also eat them. Parrotfish eat coral.

At the top of the food chain are large fish such as groupers, barracudas and sharks. They eat smaller fish, crustaceans and molluscs.

shark

barracuda

butterflyfish

grouper

parrotfish

goatfish

plankton

lobster

crab

shrimp

13

Reef Fish

Many different fish can live on a coral reef. Reefs are home to one-quarter of all marine fish species.

With such a wide variety of places to live and food to eat, many species of fish live on reefs. Fish range in size from tiny dwarf gobi, as long as your fingernail, to the largest fish in the world – the whale shark.

Many reef fish have bright colours. This provides them with good **camouflage**. Colourful spots and stripes make them difficult to see among the coral. Some fish can even change their colour to hide from **predators**. Others, such as trumpetfish, are predators that change colour to trick their prey.

basslet

Reef fish vary greatly in shape, too. The shape of a fish is often related to the way it feeds. The forceps fish has a long, thin snout that it can poke into holes and even into the stony cups of coral. Parrotfish have teeth as strong and hard as beaks for crunching up coral.

Trumpetfish hide in the coral.

Parrotfish eat coral.

A blenny hides in a hole.

The boxy trunkfish is a slow swimmer.

Living Together

Some sea creatures on the reef live very close together. They depend on each other for safety, food or shelter.

There is always a danger of predators on a reef. Some fish find safety by swimming in large schools. All their eyes look for danger so they can quickly change direction. School fish are often darker on top and lighter underneath. Darker tops make them harder to see from above, and silvery undersides are harder to see from below.

Pairs of clownfish live in the stinging tentacles of sea anemones. The clownfish don't get stung because they cover themselves in a thick layer of slime. The clownfish are protected from predators by the anemone's stingers and also eat some of its leftover food. In return, the clownfish stop other fish from attacking the anemone.

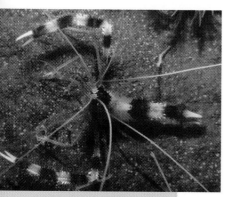

red-banded cleaner shrimp

Cleaner wrasses are very colourful, tiny fish. They get their food by removing and eating tiny creatures from the scales and mouths of bigger fish. This helps the bigger fish stay clean and free from disease. Some shrimps also do this job.

The cleaner wrasse cleans the
mouth of a coral trout.

Clownfish live in
pairs in anemones.

Remora attach
themselves to larger
fish for protection.

Schools of fish can
escape from predators.

17

Dangerous Creatures

Some creatures that live on a coral reef are very dangerous. They may be fierce hunters, or they may be armed with deadly poison.

Some of the ocean's fiercest predators visit reefs. Sharks and barracudas hunt for food on coral reefs. The tiger shark and the great white shark are fierce hunters. Both of these sharks have been known to attack people.

Many sea creatures use poison to catch and kill their prey. Sometimes these poisons can be very dangerous to humans. Cone shells are marine snails with pretty

stonefish

shells but they are predators that use darts to kill their prey. The darts contain a powerful poison that can **paralyse** people.

Jellyfish have tentacles that can give painful stings. A box jellyfish can kill a person. Some fish also have poison in spiky fins or spines along their back. The scorpionfish and the well-camouflaged stonefish are both poisonous.

Great white sharks can attack people.

Scorpionfish can easily hide in the reef.

Lionfish have venomous spines.

DID YOU KNOW?
The paralysing blue-ringed octopus has poison in its saliva.

Sea nettle jellyfish have long, stinging tentacles.

19

Reefs Under Threat

Coral reefs are fragile and they need to be protected. There are some natural threats to coral reefs, but people cause the most damage.

The crown-of-thorns starfish is a natural predator that eats coral polyps. Large numbers of crown-of-thorns starfish are destroying parts of Australia's Great Barrier Reef.

Reef fish are caught to sell to people who keep aquariums. Fishing may remove too many fish. When there are not enough fish, algae can grow over the coral.

Coral needs clear water to grow. When forests are cut down on land, erosion washes soil into the ocean. The plants inside the coral stop growing and the coral begin to die.

Pollution caused by industry and shipping can also poison coral polyps. Ships leak fuel into the water and boat anchors break off coral. Oil spills can cause huge damage as well.

Crown-of-thorns starfish destroy coral reefs.

By studying coral reefs we can learn how to protect them.

GO FACTS

DID YOU KNOW?

Coral reefs grow slowly. They only grow about 2–3 centimetres per year.

21

How Atolls Form

Coral reefs begin to form in the rich, warm waters around a volcanic island.

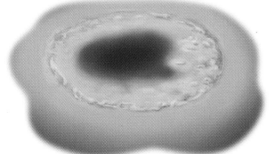

Over thousands of years, the island slowly sinks into the ocean.

An atoll (a ring of coral) remains.

Glossary

algae	water plants such as seaweed and some types of plankton
atoll	a circular coral reef that surrounds a lagoon
barrier reef	a reef that runs parallel to shore and is separated from land by deep water
camouflage	colouring that makes an animal hard to see
coral	stony skeletons of dead coral polyps
coral polyp	the animal that creates coral
crustacean	a sea animal with a hard outer shell
fringing reef	a reef that is close to shore
lagoon	a shallow area of water (near a larger body of water)
larva	the young of some animals that change form to become an adult
mollusc	a soft-bodied sea animal
paralyse	to make unable to move
plankton	microscopic plants and animals that float in the ocean
predator	an animal that hunts and eats other animals
species	animals that can breed together
tropical	being warm and wet enough for plants to grow all year long